Katie Clemons

LET'S CELEBRATE YOUR STORY

WE'RE SO

THANKFUL

A SHARED GRATITUDE JOURNAL

sourcebooks
eXplore

TO NIKLAS AND LINDEN.
MY SONG WAS SENSELESS BEFORE YOU.

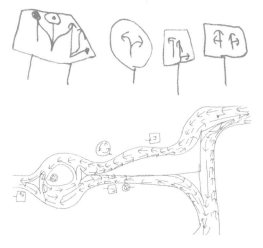

NIKLAS'S ART, AGE 4

Copyright © 2019 by Katie Clemons LLC
Cover and internal design © 2019 by Sourcebooks
Cover and internal illustrations by Maryn Arreguín

Sourcebooks and the colophon are registered trademarks of Sourcebooks.

Published by Sourcebooks eXplore, an imprint of Sourcebooks Kids
P.O. Box 4410, Naperville, Illinois 60567–4410
(630) 961-3900
sourcebookskids.com

Source of Production: Versa Press, East Peoria, Illinois, USA
Date of Production: September 2019
Run Number: 5016203

Printed and bound in the United States of America.
VP 10 9 8 7 6 5 4 3 2 1

LET'S NOTICE MOMENTS OF GRATITUDE

I FEEL CHANGE IN THE AIR whenever the aroma of chocolate cake fills our home. In a blink, we're ready for more candles, streamers, and balloons.

"Did you grow bigger?" my son Niklas asks his brother as they rub sleep from their eyes. Niklas jumps to his feet and stretches as high as he can. "I grew. I'm so big now!"

His greatest ambition at the freshly minted age of five has little to do with presents and everything to do with becoming the tallest person in our house. I reach over and wrap the birthday boy in my arms, soaking in some of his joy before he and his brother race off.

Gratitude is an attitude is a phrase I hear often. It has a nice ring, but I'm learning that being grateful is much more than saying a quick "thanks" as I dash out the door. It takes daily practice—remembering to recognize, reflect on, and celebrate the million great things in life. Sometimes the cause for gratitude is obvious.

Other times it's so fleeting we won't even know it happened.

Over the years, I've found that keeping a journal is both the easiest and most powerful way for me to cultivate a habit of appreciation, and I relish witnessing how journaling does that for other people. When we put pen to paper, we give ourselves space to reflect and ask why we feel a certain way. It makes us more receptive to good things, so we instinctively begin seeking them out, sharing them, and really feeling power behind a quick embrace or a few simple words like "thank you."

As parents and caring adults, we've got so many to-do lists, hopes, and expectations that keep us running. But I don't want to miss the joy on Niklas's face as we walk into his school because I'm worried about getting twenty-four perfect cupcakes in the door. I want to be present with my son.

This journal is my invitation for you to slow down and openly discuss timely topics and grassroots ideas about gratitude with your child or grandchild—conversations that may never surface at the dinner table or during hectic schedules. You and your child view life through lenses shaped by age and experience. A shared journal provides insight into your varied views and shared perspectives, which strengthens your relationship and appreciation.

In this journal, you'll find writing prompts that invite you and your child to become more aware of yourselves, each other, people you care about, and folks you may never meet. Some prompts make you laugh, others make you think. Some challenge you to roll up your sleeves and do something, while others invite introspection. An occasional prompt even helps your child openly communicate about difficult moments when they might not be able to see beauty and give thanks.

These six guideposts will help you get the most from your storycatching time together.

❶ BEGIN ON ANY PAGE.

You don't have to use the pages of this journal chronologically. You and your child can turn to any prompt that strikes you in the moment. Answer questions together while you chat, or pass the book back and forth, making entries in turn. Your child's stories go on pages that begin "Dear Child" or "I Write." Corresponding "My Question for You" and "You Write" pages offer you an opportunity to respond or ignite another conversation. Intermixed throughout are "Take Action" prompts that challenge you to express gratitude and spread joy in your community. Do these activities with each other whenever possible, then reflect on the corresponding questions together or encourage your child to write on their own.

❷ WELCOME IMPERFECTION.

A messy journal is infinitely better than an empty one. I cross out words, make grammar mistakes, and invent new vocabulary in my entries all the time. Without fail, my journals have a page or two where my words slowly fade as the pen I'm using runs out of ink. I've realized the best discoveries often come from letting your pen and mind wander across the page.

❸ TELL COMPLETE STORIES.

Fill this journal with as many statements like "I'm thankful for
_____" as you fancy. I've learned that there's nothing too big or too
little to appreciate, but sometimes when we talk, we get caught up
in worrying about what we perceive other people will think. I want
each of you to focus on telling your own perspective and describing
what you see and how you feel.

❹ BECOME AN ENGAGED LISTENER.

The real joy of shared journaling begins when you read the
words each other writes. It's like getting a peek inside one another's
heads and hearts. Some entries cover things you already know.
Through others, you might discover details, emotions, or entire
stories that you weren't aware of. When you read an entry, you might
feel inspired to respond immediately. But you can also walk away
and ruminate on the other person's words before you reply.

❺ PLAY.

The process of doodling, decorating, and gathering photos
or keepsakes for your journal gives you an opportunity to share
stories beyond what either of you can express in words. I love the
juxtaposition between Niklas's drawings and mine side by side.
Experiment with pens. Underline words. Draw arrows, speech
bubbles, and zigzags. Cut out and attach interesting quotations. Take
pictures together and adhere them with glue or double-sided tape.

⊘ GET AND GIVE MORE.

Your gratitude experience only begins with this journal. Join me for exclusive *We Are So Thankful* resources, including examples from my own diaries, additional posters to print and share, and creative parent-child challenges on:

KATIECLEMONS.COM/A/8B2N

Want to share your gratitude projects with me? Please drop me a note at **howdy@katieclemons.com** (I answer all my mail) or join me on social media **@katierclemons, #katieclemonsjournals,** and **#wearesothankful**.

Imagine opening this journal in ten or twenty years or giving it to your grown child. You'll see pages filled with stories and perspectives, photographs, youthful penmanship recording moments you haven't thought about in years, and best of all…reminders of how many things you have to be grateful for.

Your life is already so rich. Have the cake, and… Let's celebrate your story!

♡ Katie

HERE'S A PHOTOGRAPH OR DRAWING OF

YOU & ME

HELLO TODAY!

OUR FULL NAMES ARE

_____

_____

WE CALL EACH OTHER

_____

_____

WE'RE _____ AND _____ YEARS OLD.

WE'RE GRATEFUL FOR EACH OTHER BECAUSE

_____

_____

LET'S START THIS JOURNAL!

DATE: _____

OUR JOURNAL

GUIDELINES

1. IS OUR JOURNAL TOP SECRET OR CAN ANYONE ELSE LOOK INSIDE?

_____

_____

2. IF SOMEONE FINDS THIS JOURNAL, THEY SHOULD

☐ RETURN IT

☐ FINISH IT

☐ DESTROY IT

☐ PUBLISH IT

☐ PUT IT UP FOR AUCTION STARTING AT $_____

☐ HIDE IT IN _____

☐ _____

3. DO WE HAVE TO ANSWER PROMPTS IN NUMERICAL ORDER? ☐ YES ☐ NO

4. OUR TOP FOCUS(ES) IN THIS JOURNAL WILL BE TO

☐ EXPRESS OUR THOUGHTS

☐ USE PERFECT GRAMMAR

☐ CAPTURE MEMORIES

☐ CONNECT WITH ONE ANOTHER

☐ HAVE AN EXCUSE TO NEVER SAY OR WRITE "THANK YOU" AGAIN

☐ REFLECT ON GRATITUDE

☐ _____

☐ _____

5. HOW MUCH TIME DO WE HAVE TO WRITE BEFORE GIVING OUR JOURNAL BACK TO ONE ANOTHER?

_____

_____

6. WHAT COULD WE DO IF WE NEED MORE SPACE TO WRITE?

_____

_____

7. IS THERE A SPECIFIC DATE WHEN THIS JOURNAL
MUST BE COMPLETE?

_____

_____

8. HOW DO WE PASS OUR JOURNAL BACK AND FORTH?

_____

_____

9. HOW DO WE TELL EACH OTHER WHICH PAGE TO
TURN TO?

_____

_____

10. HOW CAN WE COMMUNICATE WHEN WE NEED AN
URGENT RESPONSE?

_____

_____

11. IF WE EVER FEEL LIKE IT'S TOO DIFFICULT TO WRITE ABOUT GRATITUDE—SUCH AS WHEN WE'RE HAVING A BAD DAY—WHAT SHOULD WE DO?

_____

_____

_____

12. ARE THERE OTHER GUIDELINES WE SHOULD ESTABLISH FOR OUR JOURNAL?

_____

_____

_____

DEAR CHILD,

WHAT'S SOMETHING I DO
THAT MAKES YOU HAPPY?

CHILD WRITES

MY QUESTION FOR YOU,

WHAT'S SOMETHING I DO
THAT MAKES YOU HAPPY?

YOU & ME

OUR JOY-FILLED FACES

YOU

ME

OUR GRUMPY FACES

YOU

ME

OUR SURPRISED FACES

YOU

ME

WE WRITE

I WRITE

I'LL NEVER FORGET HOW HAPPY
YOU WERE WHEN

YOU WRITE

I'LL NEVER FORGET HOW HAPPY
YOU WERE WHEN

DEAR CHILD,

WHAT DO YOU THINK BEING GRATEFUL MEANS?

HOW DO YOU TRY TO EXPRESS
YOUR APPRECIATION?

DO YOU HAVE A STORY OF WHEN
YOU SAW ME BEING THANKFUL?

MY QUESTION FOR YOU,

WHAT DO YOU THINK BEING GRATEFUL MEANS?

HOW DO YOU TRY TO EXPRESS
YOUR APPRECIATION?

DO YOU HAVE A STORY OF WHEN
YOU SAW ME BEING THANKFUL?

I WRITE

I REALLY ADMIRE HOW YOU

1. _____

_____

2. _____

_____

3. _____

_____

I THINK OF YOU WHENEVER

_____

_____

_____

YOU'RE REALLY GOOD AT

1. _____

2. _____

3. _____

HERE'S A PICTURE OF YOU,

MY _____!

YOU WRITE

I REALLY ADMIRE HOW YOU

1. _____

_____

2. _____

_____

3. _____

_____

I THINK OF YOU WHENEVER

_____

_____

_____

YOU'RE REALLY GOOD AT

1. _____

2. _____

3. _____

ADULT WRITES

HERE'S A PICTURE OF YOU,

MY _____ CHILD!

BRING BEAUTY TO THE ENVIRONMENT

TAKE ACTION TOGETHER

MATERIALS: PROJECT DEPENDENT

TIME INVESTMENT: 15 MINUTES MINIMUM

LOCATION: A PUBLIC SPACE

PROJECT: SPEND SOME TIME MAKING A PUBLIC SPACE IN YOUR COMMUNITY NICER, AND INVITE PEOPLE TO JOIN YOU. YOU COULD PULL WEEDS, PICK UP TRASH, PAINT A MURAL, WASH WINDOWS AND DOORS, OR LEARN TO REPAIR SOMETHING.

REFLECTIONS

I WRITE

TASK DATE:_____

PROJECT:_____

LOCATION:_____

PARTICIPANTS:_____

CHILD WRITES

WE CHOSE TO _____ BECAUSE

WHEN WE WERE DONE,
IT LOOKED LIKE

BEFORE WE STARTED,
THE SPACE LOOKED LIKE

COMPLETING THIS PROJECT MADE ME FEEL

I THINK IT MADE _____ FEEL _____

IF WE WERE TO DO THIS PROJECT OVER, WE WOULD

I BELIEVE IT [IS/ISN'T] IMPORTANT TO TAKE CARE
OF OUR PUBLIC SPACES BECAUSE

WE GIVE OUR PROJECT ☆☆☆☆☆ STARS!

DATE

I WRITE

TODAY I'M NOTICING

THE SOUND OF

THE SMELL OF

THE SIGHT OF

THE TASTE OF

THE FEEL OF

CHILD WRITES

YOU WRITE

TODAY I'M NOTICING

THE SOUND OF

THE SMELL OF

THE SIGHT OF

THE FEEL OF

THE TASTE OF

I WRITE

PEOPLE WHO HELPED ME THIS WEEK

1

2

3

4

5

CHILD WRITES

YOU WRITE

PEOPLE WHO HELPED ME THIS WEEK

1

2

3

4

5

DEAR CHILD,

TELL ME ALL ABOUT SOMEONE YOU ADMIRE.

WHAT'S THE #1 REASON THIS PERSON
INSPIRES YOU SO MUCH?

ADD AN INSPIRATIONAL QUOTE

CHILD WRITES

HOW IS OUR COMMUNITY OR WORLD A
BETTER PLACE BECAUSE OF THIS PERSON?

TELL ME ABOUT AN OBSTACLE THIS
PERSON HAD TO OVERCOME.

KEEP GOING

DO YOU THINK YOU COULD DO THAT?

DO YOU THINK THIS PERSON EVER MADE
MISTAKES OR FELT LIKE THEY'D FAILED?
WHY WOULD THEY KEEP GOING?

DESCRIBE A FEW WAYS YOU'RE
SIMILAR TO THIS PERSON.

❶

❷

❸

HOW COULD YOU BECOME MORE
LIKE THIS PERSON?

FUTURE ME, AGE _____

MY QUESTION FOR YOU,

WHAT ARE YOUR THOUGHTS ON
WHAT I'VE WRITTEN ABOUT
THE PERSON I ADMIRE?

WHICH TRAITS DO I SHARE WITH THEM?

1.

2.

3.

YOU & ME

WE ALWAYS ENJOY

TIME ALONE TO

YOU

ME

TIME TOGETHER TO

YOU

ME

TIME WITH FAMILY OR FRIENDS TO

YOU

ME

WE WRITE

MY QUESTION FOR YOU,

TELL ME ALL ABOUT SOMEONE YOU ADMIRE.

WHAT'S THE #1 REASON THIS PERSON
INSPIRES YOU SO MUCH?

ADD AN INSPIRATIONAL QUOTE

ADULT WRITES

HOW IS OUR COMMUNITY OR WORLD A
BETTER PLACE BECAUSE OF THIS PERSON?

TELL ME ABOUT AN OBSTACLE THIS
PERSON HAD TO OVERCOME.

KEEP GOING

DO YOU THINK YOU COULD DO THAT?

DO YOU THINK THIS PERSON EVER MADE
MISTAKES OR FELT LIKE THEY'D FAILED?
WHY WOULD THEY KEEP GOING?

DESCRIBE A FEW WAYS YOU'RE
SIMILAR TO THIS PERSON.

1

2

3

HOW COULD YOU BECOME MORE LIKE THIS PERSON?

FUTURE ME, AGE _____

DEAR CHILD,

WHAT ARE YOUR THOUGHTS ON WHAT I'VE WRITTEN ABOUT THE PERSON I ADMIRE?

WHICH TRAITS DO I SHARE WITH THEM?

1.

2.

3.

DATE

YOU ME

SOMETHING KIND WE CAN SAY TO
OURSELVES ON A DIFFICULT DAY

YOU WRITE

I WRITE

WE WRITE

HELP AT HOME
TAKE ACTION

MATERIALS: NONE

TIME INVESTMENT: 10 MINUTES

LOCATION: AT HOME

WHO: CHILD

PROJECT: COMPLETE A CHORE AT HOME THAT YOU DON'T NORMALLY DO. BE ANONYMOUS IF YOU'D LIKE.

IDEAS: GRAB THE VACUUM, EMPTY EVERY TRASHCAN, CLEAN THE SINK, PUT AWAY CLEAN CLOTHES, OR DUST.

REFLECTIONS
I WRITE

TASK DATE: _____

CHORE: _____

_____ NORMALLY DOES THIS JOB.

IT [WAS/WASN'T] DIFFICULT FOR ME TO COMPLETE.

CHILD WRITES

☐ I DECIDED TO KEEP MY PROJECT A SECRET BECAUSE

_____

☐ I DIDN'T KEEP MY PROJECT A SECRET BECAUSE

_____

I WANTED TO HELP THIS PERSON WITH THE CHORE
BECAUSE _____

_____

WHEN I WAS FINISHED, THE HOUSE LOOKED

_____

KNOWING THAT I MADE THAT PERSON'S DAY EASIER,
I FEEL _____

OTHER WAYS I COULD HELP AROUND THE HOUSE
INCLUDE _____

_____

I GIVE MY PROJECT ☆☆☆☆☆ STARS!

DATE

I WRITE

I'M GLAD THE WORLD HAS MY FAVORITE

ICE CREAM

BREAKFAST FOOD

CANDY

WEBSITE

MOVIE

BOOK

YOU WRITE

I'M GLAD THE WORLD HAS MY FAVORITE

BREAKFAST FOOD

ICE CREAM

CANDY

WEBSITE

MOVIE

BOOK

DEAR CHILD,

I HAVE A QUESTION FOR YOU

CHILD WRITES

I WRITE

WAYS THAT YOU AND I ARE

DIFFERENT FROM
ONE ANOTHER

❶

❷

❸

THE SAME AS
EACH OTHER

❶

❷

❸

I LOVE HOW OUR DIFFERENCES AND
COMMONALITIES MAKE OUR RELATIONSHIP

YOU WRITE

WAYS THAT YOU AND I ARE

DIFFERENT FROM
ONE ANOTHER

1

2

3

THE SAME AS
EACH OTHER

1

2

3

I LOVE HOW OUR DIFFERENCES AND
COMMONALITIES MAKE OUR RELATIONSHIP

I WRITE

ONE OF THE BEST GIFTS I EVER RECEIVED

FROM:

ONE OF THE BEST GIFTS I EVER GAVE

TO:

YOU WRITE

ONE OF THE BEST GIFTS I EVER RECEIVED

FROM:

ONE OF THE BEST GIFTS I EVER GAVE

TO:

PLANT KINDNESS

DATE

NAME:
KIND WORDS:

NAME:
KIND WORDS:

NAME:
KIND WORDS:

NAME:
KIND WORDS:

NAME:
KIND WORDS:

NAME:
KIND WORDS:

NAME:
KIND WORDS:

NAME:
KIND WORDS:

KIND WORDS WE'D
LIKE TO GIVE OTHERS

YOU & ME

WE WRITE

55

DEAR CHILD,

TELL ME ABOUT A RELATIVE
YOU LOVE AND APPRECIATE.

CHILD WRITES

ADD A
PICTURE!

MY QUESTION FOR YOU,

TELL ME ABOUT A RELATIVE
THAT I DIDN'T GET TO KNOW WELL.

ADULT WRITES

DATE

ADD A
PICTURE!

DEAR CHILD,

WHAT'S SOMETHING YOU WORRY ABOUT?

WHY DOES THIS BOTHER YOU?

CHILD WRITES

DO YOU HAVE ANY IDEAS ON HOW YOU
COULD EASE YOUR CONCERNS?

ARE THERE WAYS YOU'D LIKE ME TO HELP?

MY QUESTION FOR YOU,

WHAT ARE YOUR THOUGHTS ON
WHAT WORRIES ME?

DO YOU HAVE ANY IDEAS ON HOW I COULD
WORRY LESS? MAYBE WITH YOUR HELP?

WHAT DO YOU DO WHEN
SOMETHING CONCERNS YOU?

I'LL ALWAYS TELL YOU

THANK YOU!

DEAR CHILD,

TELL ME ABOUT A TIME WHEN YOU DID
SOMETHING KIND FOR ANOTHER PERSON,
EVEN WHEN YOU DIDN'T HAVE TO.

HOW DID IT MAKE YOU FEEL?

DO YOU THINK THERE'S SOMEONE ELSE
YOU COULD HELP IN A SIMILAR WAY?

CHILD WRITES

MY QUESTION FOR YOU,

TELL ME ABOUT A TIME WHEN YOU DID
SOMETHING KIND FOR ANOTHER PERSON,
EVEN WHEN YOU DIDN'T HAVE TO.

HOW DID IT MAKE YOU FEEL?

DO YOU THINK THERE'S SOMEONE ELSE
YOU COULD HELP IN A SIMILAR WAY?

ADULT WRITES

YOU & ME

THREE THINGS THAT MAKE US BELLY-LAUGH WITH JOY.

YOU

1

2

3

ME

1

2

3

LOL

WE WRITE

YOU & ME

SOMETHING WE GIVE TO PEOPLE WE LOVE

YOU

ME

SOMETHING WE DO FOR THE ENVIRONMENT

YOU

ME

SOMETHING WE HELP STRANGERS WITH

YOU

ME

WE WRITE   69

WE'RE GRATEFUL
FOR INCREDIBLE
THINGS WE'VE
DONE TOGETHER.

WE WRITE

AWESOME

WE LOOK
FORWARD TO
WONDERFUL THINGS
WE STILL NEED
TO DO TOGETHER.

YOU WRITE

I APPRECIATE HOW MOST MORNINGS YOU

I'M GRATEFUL THAT MOST EVENINGS YOU

I WRITE

I APPRECIATE HOW MOST MORNINGS YOU

I'M GRATEFUL THAT MOST EVENINGS YOU

WE WRITE

YOU WRITE

EVERY YEAR I LOOK FORWARD TO

I WRITE

EVERY YEAR I LOOK FORWARD TO

YOU WRITE

HERE'S AN INSPIRING QUOTATION, PASSAGE, OR POEM I FOUND

I'M ADDING IT TO OUR JOURNAL BECAUSE

I WRITE

HERE'S AN INSPIRING QUOTATION, PASSAGE, OR POEM I FOUND

I'M ADDING IT TO OUR JOURNAL BECAUSE

SPREAD KINDNESS GESTURES

TAKE ACTION TOGETHER

MATERIALS: POSTER ON NEXT PAGE, SCISSORS, TAPE, CRAYONS OR MARKERS, OTHER EMBELLISHMENTS (OPTIONAL)

TIME INVESTMENT: 5 MINUTES

LOCATION: A PUBLIC SPACE

PROJECT: SHARE JOY BY SHARING THIS TEAR-APART POSTER. CUT ALONG THE DOTTED LINES. THEN DECORATE IT AND HANG IT IN A PUBLIC SPACE WHERE PEOPLE CAN TEAR OFF THE TAG THEY NEED.

CHILD WRITES

KINDNESS CAN CHANGE EVERYTHING

TEAR OFF A TAG. GIVE IT AWAY.

YOU'VE GOT THIS.

YOU MAKE MY
LIFE RICHER.

I APPRECIATE YOU.

THANK YOU!

I BELIEVE IN YOU.

THANK YOU FOR
HELPING ME.

YOU CAN DO IT.

THANK YOU
FOR BEING YOU.

YOU ARE LOVED.

PLEASE FORGIVE ME.

REFLECTIONS

I WRITE

PROJECT DATE: _____

PARTICIPANTS: _____

WE HUNG OUR POSTER AT _____

I THINK IT'S A GOOD PLACE FOR THIS MESSAGE

BECAUSE _____

IF I WERE TO TEAR OFF A TAG TO GIVE SOMEONE,

I'D WANT _____ BECAUSE

_____

I THINK IT'S IMPORTANT TO SPREAD KINDNESS

BECAUSE _____

WE [HAVE/HAVEN'T] SEEN IF ANYONE HAS TAKEN

A MESSAGE YET.

WE GIVE OUR PROJECT ☆☆☆☆☆ STARS!

MY QUESTION FOR YOU,

CHILD WRITES
QUESTION HERE

?

ADULT WRITES

YOU WRITE

EACH SEASON, I ENJOY

SPRING

SUMMER

FALL

WINTER

ADULT WRITES

I WRITE

EACH SEASON, I ENJOY

SPRING

SUMMER

FALL

WINTER

DEAR CHILD,

TELL ME ABOUT AN ACTIVITY THAT
YOU LOVE TO PARTICIPATE IN.

WHAT DO YOU ENJOY ABOUT IT?

DRAW ME A PICTURE

CHILD WRITES

WHO ARE THE PEOPLE WHO HELP MAKE
THIS EXPERIENCE POSSIBLE FOR YOU?

WHY DO YOU THINK THEY INVEST
THEMSELVES IN THIS ACTIVITY?

HOW DO YOU OR HOW COULD YOU EXPRESS
YOUR APPRECIATION TO THEM?

WHY DO YOU THINK THAT'S
AN IMPORTANT THING TO DO?

HAVE YOU EVER HELPED OTHERS
IN THIS ACTIVITY?

HOW DID THAT MAKE YOU FEEL?

MY QUESTION FOR YOU,

WHAT ARE YOUR THOUGHTS ON WHAT I JUST WROTE
ABOUT THE ACTIVITY I LOVE?

WHY DO YOU THINK IT'S IMPORTANT TO
THANK PEOPLE WHO INVEST TIME INTO
THINGS THAT MATTER TO US?

TELL ME ABOUT AN ACTIVITY YOU REALLY
ENJOYED WHEN YOU WERE MY AGE.

DRAW ME A PICTURE.

WHO HELPED MAKE THIS EXPERIENCE
POSSIBLE FOR YOU?

DEAR CHILD,

TELL ME ABOUT A FAVORITE TEACHER.

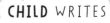

CHILD WRITES

WHAT HAS THAT PERSON HELPED
YOU LEARN? HOW?

WHY DO YOU THINK THIS PERSON
HAS SUPPORTED YOU SO MUCH?

MY QUESTION FOR YOU,

TELL ME ABOUT A FAVORITE TEACHER.

ADULT WRITES

WHAT DID THAT PERSON HELP
YOU LEARN? HOW?

HOW DID THAT PERSON INFLUENCE
WHO YOU ARE TODAY?

I WRITE

MY FAVORITE HOLIDAY IS

BECAUSE

THE CELEBRATION

SMELLS LIKE

TASTES LIKE

LOOKS LIKE

SOUNDS LIKE

FEELS LIKE

CHILD WRITES

THESE PEOPLE MAKE THE HOLIDAY MAGICAL

HERE'S WHY I THINK THEY DO IT

I TRY TO MAKE THIS HOLIDAY NICER
FOR PEOPLE I LOVE BY

I COULD MAKE IT A BETTER DAY
FOR PEOPLE I'VE NEVER MET BY

MY FAVORITE HOLIDAY IS

BECAUSE

THE CELEBRATION

SMELLS LIKE

TASTES LIKE

LOOKS LIKE

SOUNDS LIKE

FEELS LIKE

THESE PEOPLE MAKE THE HOLIDAY MAGICAL

HERE'S WHY I THINK THEY DO IT

I TRY TO MAKE THIS HOLIDAY NICER
FOR PEOPLE I LOVE BY

I COULD MAKE IT A BETTER DAY
FOR PEOPLE I'VE NEVER MET BY

I WRITE

HERE'S A LIST OF THINGS I'M GLAD I CAN DO

AND HERE'S ONE THING I
HAVEN'T BEEN ABLE TO DO...YET!

YOU WRITE

HERE'S A LIST OF THINGS I'M GLAD I CAN DO

AND HERE'S ONE THING I
HAVEN'T BEEN ABLE TO DO...YET!

MAKE A CHEER TRAIL

TAKE ACTION TOGETHER

MATERIALS: SIDEWALK CHALK

TIME INVESTMENT: 20-60 MINUTES

LOCATION: ANYWHERE IT'S SAFE TO WRITE ON THE SIDEWALK, SUCH AS IN FRONT OF YOUR HOUSE, YOUR DRIVEWAY, OR EVEN THE SIDEWALK AROUND A LOCAL SENIOR CENTER OR HOSPITAL.

PROJECT: DECORATE THE SIDEWALKS WITH CHALK. DRAW COLORFUL PICTURES. WRITE FRIENDLY NOTES OR WORDS OF ENCOURAGEMENT. INVITE OTHERS TO CONTRIBUTE. IF THERE'S TOO MUCH SNOW OR RAIN, HOW COULD YOU BRING THE JOY INSIDE?

REFLECTIONS
I WRITE

PROJECT DATE: _____

LOCATION: _____

PARTICIPANTS: _____

HERE'S WHAT WE DECIDED TO DO

_____

WHEN WE WERE FINISHED, EVERYTHING LOOKED

_____

COMPLETING THIS PROJECT MADE ME FEEL

_____

I LIKED WORKING TOGETHER BECAUSE

_____

I THINK OUR PROJECT MADE OTHER PEOPLE FEEL

_____

WE GIVE OUR PROJECT ☆☆☆☆☆ STARS!

DATE

MY QUESTION FOR YOU,

WILL YOU TEACH
ME HOW TO

CHILD WRITES
QUESTION HERE

?

ADULT WRITES

YOU & ME

MOMENTS WE'VE ENJOYED TOGETHER

TODAY

YOU

ME

THIS WEEK

YOU

ME

THIS YEAR

YOU

ME

WE WRITE   101

YOU & ME

NICE!

DATE

DEAR CHILD,

TELL ME ABOUT SOMETHING THAT
MAKES YOU FEEL ASHAMED OR GUILTY.

WHY DO YOU THINK IT MAKES
YOU FEEL THAT WAY?

DO YOU THINK THERE'S A WAY TO FIND
GRATITUDE IN THIS SITUATION?

MY QUESTION FOR YOU,

TELL ME ABOUT SOMETHING THAT MAKES YOU FEEL ASHAMED OR GUILTY.

WHY DO YOU THINK IT MAKES YOU FEEL THAT WAY?

DO YOU THINK THERE'S A WAY TO FIND GRATITUDE IN THIS SITUATION?

YOU & ME

WE LOVE THIS WEEKEND BREAKFAST

YOU

ME

PASS US MORE OF THIS SNACK

YOU

ME

GIVE US SECONDS WHEN THIS IS FOR DINNER

YOU

ME

  **WE** WRITE

YOU WRITE

I'M REALLY GRATEFUL THAT YOU DON'T

I WRITE

I'M REALLY GRATEFUL THAT YOU DON'T

YOU WRITE

A SELF-PORTRAIT

ADULT WRITES

I LOVE MY BODY JUST HOW IT IS BECAUSE

1. _____

2. _____

3. _____

I SMILE A LOT WHEN

_____

I'M PROUD OF MYSELF FOR

_____

THE BEST PART OF BEING MY AGE IS

_____

THE BEST $_____ I EVER
SPENT ON MYSELF WAS

_____

MY PERSONAL THEME SONG COULD BE

_____

I WRITE

A SELF-PORTRAIT

I LOVE MY BODY JUST HOW IT IS BECAUSE

1. ....

2. ....

3. ....

I SMILE A LOT WHEN

....

I'M PROUD OF MYSELF FOR

....

THE BEST PART OF BEING MY AGE IS

....

THE BEST $............ I EVER
SPENT ON MYSELF WAS

....

MY PERSONAL THEME SONG COULD BE

....

GO ON A GRATITUDE SCAVENGER HUNT

TAKE ACTION TOGETHER

MATERIALS: PENCIL OR PEN, THIS JOURNAL

TIME INVESTMENT: 30-60 MINUTES

LOCATION: AROUND THE NEIGHBORHOOD

PROJECT: EXPLORE THE OUTDOORS WITH THIS GRATITUDE LIST AS YOUR GUIDE, AND RECORD YOUR FINDINGS.

SCAVENGER HUNT
I WRITE

PROJECT DATE: _____

LOCATION: _____

PARTICIPANTS: _____

MAP IT OUT!

CHILD WRITES

☐ SOMETHING THAT MAKES US FEEL LIKE WE'RE A PART OF SOMETHING

_____

_____

☐ SOMETHING THAT MAKES US SMILE

_____

_____

☐ SOMETHING THAT HELPS PEOPLE

_____

_____

☐ SOMETHING THAT REPRESENTS OUR COUNTRY, COMMUNITY, OR CULTURE

_____

_____

☐ SOMETHING THAT SOMEONE WORKED HARD TO CREATE

_____

_____

☐ SOMETHING THAT SMELLS AMAZING

_____

_____

☐ SOMETHING THAT MAKES A BEAUTIFUL SOUND

_____

_____

☐ SOMETHING WE HAVE TO GET ON OUR KNEES
TO SEE

_____

_____

☐ SOMETHING THAT WE CAN GIVE TO SOMEONE

_____

_____

☐ SOMETHING IN OUR FAVORITE COLORS

_____

_____

CHILD WRITES

☐ SOMETHING COLD TO THE TOUCH

☐ SOMETHING THAT WELCOMES STRANGERS

☐ SOMETHING WE DON'T USUALLY NOTICE

☐ SOMETHING THAT'S EASY TO COMPLAIN ABOUT
BUT MAKES OUR COMMUNITY OR WORLD BETTER

☐ SOMETHING THAT

HERE'S A PICTURE OF
YOU & ME
IN OUR COMMUNITY

WE GIVE THIS PLACE ☆☆☆☆☆ STARS!

WE WRITE

AROUND HERE, WE
SPEND A LOT OF TIME

IT'S BEEN A WHILE
SINCE WE'VE

IF OUR COMMUNITY
HAD A SOUNDTRACK,
IT'D BE CALLED

IT WOULD INCLUDE
THESE SONGS

1.

2.

THE COVER WOULD
LOOK LIKE

THE VOLUME
CONTROL WOULD
BE ADJUSTED TO

EVERYONE WOULD EAT _____
WHILE LISTENING.

YOU WRITE

HERE'S A LIST OF THINGS I'M THANKFUL FOR TODAY

I WRITE

HERE'S A LIST OF THINGS I'M THANKFUL FOR TODAY

WE WRITE

YOU & ME

HOW WE EXPRESS APPRECIATION TOWARD

OUR FRIENDS

YOU

ME

OUR TEACHERS, ROLE MODELS, OR MENTORS

YOU

ME

EACH OTHER

YOU

ME

WE WRITE

119

DEAR _____.

I HAVE A QUESTION FOR YOU.

_____

_____

WE WRITE

HANG A SURPRISE APPRECIATION POSTER

TAKE ACTION TOGETHER

MATERIALS: BLANK PIECE OF PAPER, TAPE, CRAYONS OR MARKERS, OTHER EMBELLISHMENTS (OPTIONAL)

TIME INVESTMENT: 5 MINUTES

LOCATION: ANYWHERE YOU CAN SHOW YOUR APPRECIATION AT HOME OR IN YOUR COMMUNITY

PROJECT: SOMETIMES IT'S NICE TO SURPRISE PEOPLE WITH UNANTICIPATED GRATITUDE. DECORATE YOUR PAGE WITH A POSITIVE MESSAGE OF THANKS. BRING IT TO YOUR FAVORITE PERSON, HANG IT ON YOUR SISTER'S DOOR, OR SLIP IT ONTO YOUR FAVORITE TEACHER'S DESK WHEN THEY'RE NOT LOOKING.

IDEA: OTHER CANDIDATES TO CONSIDER MIGHT INCLUDE YOUR PRINCIPAL, MAYOR, FAMILY MEMBER, STREET CLEANER, WAITER, CHARITY ORGANIZER, FIREFIGHTER, EXTRACURRICULAR LEADER, COACH, CONSTRUCTION WORKER, MAIL CARRIER, OR POLICE OFFICER.

CHILD WRITES

REFLECTIONS
I WRITE

PROJECT DATE: ....

LOCATION: ....

PARTICIPANTS: ....

HERE'S WHAT WE DECIDED TO DO

....

WE CHOSE TO SURPRISE THIS PERSON BECAUSE

....

☐ SOMEONE SAW US HANG THE POSTER BUT DIDN'T SAY ANYTHING.

☐ SOMEONE SAW US HANG THE POSTER AND SAID

....

☐ NO ONE KNOWS WE DID IT!

LEAVING THIS THANK YOU MESSAGE MADE ME FEEL

....

WE GIVE OUR PROJECT ☆☆☆☆☆ STARS!

YOU & ME

SOMETHING KIND WE CAN SAY TO
EACH OTHER ON A CHALLENGING DAY.

YOU

ME

WE WRITE

WAYS WE CAN EXPRESS THANKS

1. _____
2. _____
3. _____
4. _____
5. _____

HERE'S A WAY PEOPLE COMMUNICATE APPRECIATION IN ANOTHER CULTURE OR LANGUAGE

_____
_____
_____
_____
_____
_____
_____

YOU WRITE

THIS IS MY FAMILY

I'M GRATEFUL FOR EACH OF THESE INDIVIDUALS BECAUSE

_____

_____

_____

_____

THEY MAKE ME FEEL

SHOULD I TELL THEM?   ☐ YES   ☐ NO

I WRITE

THIS IS MY FAMILY

I'M GRATEFUL FOR EACH OF THESE INDIVIDUALS BECAUSE

_____

_____

_____

_____

THEY MAKE ME FEEL

SHOULD I TELL THEM? ☐ YES ☐ NO

HERE'S A PICTURE OF
YOU & ME
SPREADING JOY

WE WRITE

YOU & ME

WE COULD SPEND THE WHOLE WEEKEND WITH OUR
FAMILY DOING NOTHING BUT

YOU WRITE

I WRITE

WE WRITE

YOU WRITE

THANK YOU FOR ALWAYS

I WRITE

THANK YOU FOR ALWAYS

WE WRITE

SPREAD GRATITUDE OUR WAY

TAKE ACTION TOGETHER

HERE'S SOMETHING SIMPLE WE COULD DO THIS WEEK TO MAKE OTHER PEOPLE SMILE.

PROJECT TITLE: _____

MATERIALS: _____

TIME INVESTMENT: _____

LOCATION: _____

PROJECT DESCRIPTION: _____
_____

REFLECTIONS

I WRITE

TASK DATE: _____

LOCATION: _____

PARTICIPANTS: _____

WE CHOSE OUR PROJECT BECAUSE: _____
_____

WE GIVE OUR PROJECT ☆☆☆☆☆ STARS!

CHILD WRITES   131

YOU WRITE

RIGHT NOW, I'M GRATEFUL FOR

THIS PERSON

THIS PLACE

THIS EVERYDAY OBJECT

THIS ACTIVITY ON THE CALENDAR

THIS PART OF ME

THIS

I WRITE

RIGHT NOW, I'M GRATEFUL FOR

THIS PERSON

THIS PLACE

THIS EVERYDAY OBJECT

THIS ACTIVITY ON THE CALENDAR

THIS PART OF ME

THIS

YOU WRITE

I HOPE THAT ONE DAY YOU GET THE CHANCE TO

_____

_____

_____

_____

SOMETIMES THINGS TURN OUT BETTER THAN YOU
EXPECT. WHEN THAT HAPPENS, REMEMBER TO THANK

_____

_____

_____

WHEN THINGS DON'T GO AS
YOU PLANNED, REMEMBER

_____

_____

_____

I WRITE

I HOPE THAT ONE DAY YOU GET THE CHANCE TO

_____

_____

_____

_____

SOMETIMES THINGS TURN OUT BETTER THAN YOU
EXPECT. WHEN THAT HAPPENS, YOU'VE TAUGHT ME

_____

_____

_____

WHEN THINGS DON'T GO AS WE PLAN,
I APPRECIATE YOUR ADVICE TO

_____

_____

_____

YOU WRITE

I NEVER WANT TO FORGET HOW YOU

I WRITE

I NEVER WANT TO FORGET HOW YOU

WE WRITE

YOU & ME

A FEW THINGS OTHER PEOPLE DID THIS
PAST WEEK THAT MADE US GRATEFUL

YOU

ME

GIVE A GIFT

TAKE ACTION TOGETHER

MATERIALS: SMALL GIFT

TIME INVESTMENT: 15 MINUTES MINIMUM

PROJECT: MAKE OR BUY A SMALL GIFT FOR SOMEONE OUTSIDE OF YOUR FAMILY WHO HELPS YOU. DELIVER YOUR GIFT WITH A HUGE THANK YOU.

REFLECTIONS

I WRITE

TASK DATE: _____

RECIPIENT: _____

GIFT: _____

PARTICIPANTS: _____

I'M SO GRATEFUL FOR _____ BECAUSE

CHILD WRITES

WE DECIDED TO SURPRISE THIS PERSON WITH

_____

THE RECIPIENT RESPONDED BY _____

_____

I THINK OUR GESTURE MATTERED TO THIS PERSON

BECAUSE _____

_____

EXPRESSING GRATITUDE MADE ME FEEL

_____

_____

HERE'S A PICTURE!

WE GIVE OUR PROJECT ☆☆☆☆☆ STARS!

I WRITE

I'M GRATEFUL FOR YOU, BECAUSE BY KEEPING THIS
JOURNAL TOGETHER, I FEEL LIKE WE

YOU WRITE

I'M GRATEFUL FOR YOU, MY CHILD, BECAUSE BY
KEEPING THIS JOURNAL TOGETHER, I FEEL LIKE WE

WE WRITE

DEAR CHILD,

TELL ME WHAT'S ON YOUR MIND.

HERE'S A PICTURE OF

YOU & ME

THANKFUL FOR _____ !

WE WRITE

DEAR CHILD,

YAHOO! WE'VE COMPLETED OUR JOURNAL.
IT WAS

WHAT DID YOU ENJOY ABOUT WRITING TOGETHER?

HOW SHOULD WE CELEBRATE OUR
JOURNAL'S COMPLETION?

IS THERE A LAST ACT OF KINDNESS WE
SHOULD RECORD IN THIS JOURNAL?
MAYBE WE COULD SURPRISE SOMEONE.

WHAT SHOULD WE DO WITH THIS JOURNAL?

 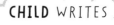

LET'S CELEBRATE YOUR STORY!

I believe that your story is one of the most
meaningful gifts you can give yourself and
the people you love. Thank you for entrusting
me and this journal with your adventures.
If you loved writing in these pages, let's celebrate
more of your story with my other books. They're
just as empowering and, well, awesome!

♡ Katie

BETWEEN **MOM** AND **ME**: A Mother & Son Keepsake Journal

LOVE, **MOM** AND **ME**: A Mother & Daughter Keepsake Journal

BETWEEN **DAD** AND **ME**: A Father & Son Keepsake Journal

LOVE, **DAD** AND **ME**: A Father & Daughter Keepsake Journal

AWAITING YOU: A Pregnancy Journal

DISCOVER EVEN MORE KATIE CLEMONS
JOURNALS AT **KATIECLEMONS.COM**!